www.clfpublishing.org
909.315.3161

Copyright © 2022 by Cassundra White-Elliott.

All rights reserved. No portion of this book may be reproduced, stored in a retrieval system, or transmitted by any form or any means electronically, photocopied, recorded, or any other except for brief quotations in printed reviews, without the prior permission of the publisher.

Cover design by Senir Design. Contact info: info@senirdesign.com

Illustrations by Mariya Akram via Fivver.com

ISBN #978-1-945102-80-6

Printed in the United States of America.

Dedication

This book is dedicated to all the students at Excellence Academy.

Every Wednesday evening, James and his little sister Cindy stay at home with their babysitter Kim, while their parents go out to dinner with friends. After they finish their homework, they usually sit in the living room and find a good movie to watch together, while eating their after-dinner snacks. This Wednesday, they decided to watch a comedy show their cousins had told them about.

James and Cindy get so excited by the comedy show they are watching that they begin laughing very hard. They are having so much fun that they stand up on the couch and begin jumping. After taking a big leap into the air, Cindy bumps into James. Then, James bumps into a lamp, knocking it onto the floor. The lamp crashes hard, and it breaks.

Kim is down the hall in the bathroom. She hears the noise and runs into the living room to see what is going on. James is attempting to pick up the broken pieces of the lamp. Cindy is busy cleaning up the snacks that have spilled all over the carpet. "What happened in here?" Kim yells. Neither of the children answers her.

"Answer me!" Kim yells.

James looks at Kim and says, "We were just watching tv and the lamp fell over."

"The lamp fell by itself?" Kim asks.

"Yes," James insists.

"Is that true?" Kim asks Cindy.

Cindy doesn't answer. She holds her head down and begins crying.

Kim sends the children to bed, and she cleans up the mess. When the children's parents return home, Kim tells them what happened. The next morning, James and Cindy sit at the table, eating breakfast with their parents. No one mentions the broken lamp. After breakfast, the children leave for school.

At school that day, James is in class listening to his teacher Mr. Lee go over the science lesson. When he is finished, Mr. Lee asks all the students for their homework. One of James' classmates says, "I don't have mine, Mr. Lee." Mr. Lee has a disappointed look on his face. He looks at the student and asks, "Scott, did you forget your homework again?" Scott answers, "No. My baby brother spilled his milk on it." "I thought your mother and brother were away taking care of your sick grandma," Mr. Lee says. "Uh, yeah," Scott says in a low voice. "Scott, it is never good to lie. It's always best to tell the truth."

Mr. Lee explains how lies can lead to people being hurt by receiving false information. Scott stands up and apologizes to Mr. Lee and the class. Meanwhile, the rest of the students turn in their homework assignments. Later, they go out for lunch and play time.

Later that evening, James and his family are having dinner. His father asks about the broken lamp and tells his children what Kim the babysitter told him and his wife. James says, "I know I shouldn't have lied about the lamp. I just didn't want to get in trouble for jumping on the couch and breaking it." His mother looked at him and then to Cindy. "You are not setting a good example for your sister when you lie. It's always best to tell the truth, even if you must suffer the consequences of your actions." "Yes, ma'am," James says.

Telling the truth when you have done something wrong may not always be the easiest thing to do, especially if you know you may get into trouble. But, the truth is always better than a lie. Telling the truth can sometimes prevent other bad things from happening. And, you never know, it may not be as bad as you think. After all, parents, teachers, and other adults make mistakes too.

www.ingramcontent.com/pod-product-compliance
Lightning Source LLC
Chambersburg PA
CBHW040121170426
42813CB00110B/2914